My Life in the Poetry Lane

George E. Valler

BookLocker
Trenton, Georgia

Copyright © 2023 George E. Valler

Print ISBN: 978-1-958890-34-9
Ebook ISBN: 979-8-88531-537-1

All rights reserved. No part of this publication may be reproduced, stored in a retrieval system, or transmitted in any form or by any means, electronic, mechanical, recording or otherwise, without the prior written permission of the author.

Published by BookLocker.com, Inc., Trenton, Georgia.

Printed on acid-free paper.

The narrative within this book is based on actual events in the author's life.

BookLocker.com, Inc.
2023

First Edition

Library of Congress Cataloguing in Publication Data
Valler, George E.
My Life in the Poetry Lane by George E. Valler
Library of Congress Control Number: 2023911893

This book isn't heavy but you'll find it hard to put down

CHAPTER 1

MY LIFE IN THE POETRY LANE

In the beginning - if you are to come with me on a journey through my poetry book, let us start with a million to one chance that I personally had. Not many, if any, could say they have had a million to one happening.
It all occurred a few years ago, so I thought I should put the whole event into verse.

They say a chance in a million
for some things you just can't believe
let's add another few million
I know that's hard to perceive.

Let's set the scene, its Guy Fawkes,
an evening of flaming delight
with the burning of fire and fireworks
to make the evening burn bright.

Guy Fawkes up high on a wooden pyre
engulfed now all in flame
and a pyrotechnic spitting sky
burns out his claim to fame.

But all too soon the night has closed
the midnight bell has tolled the day
and duffle up in furry coats
we are now on our way.

George E. Valler

As we walked the lonely lane,
the gates of the park now closed
and darkness clothed, its blanket shroud,
into the black the night unfolds.

The footbridge stretches out before
oily river waters flow
into the distance of the village dark
is the path that we must go.

The village lost in silent sleep,
slumber on the night away
whilst family we, with glowing torch,
go on into the grey.

Then all at once, so suddenly,
way out, don't ask me why,
a lonely rocket, fiery tail,
burst crystal light into the sky.

A spluttered moment, silence descends,
the quiet now all around.
but a lonely rocket fired high,
can now only come to ground.

The family gathered, the lowly torch,
as we continued into the night
unaware as we all were,
what was to be my plight.

My Life in The Poetry Lane

They say that I am accident prone,
if it happens it will be me,
and in the blackened stillness night
a spent rocket falling free.

It couldn't have been a smaller one,
that spurts flame momentarily.
It had to be a larger one
no expense spared, so you see.

The first I knew from out the sky
and with darkness all around
my hand reached out, my bleeding head,
whilst the blaggard fell to ground.

Look out, what's up, don't stop like that.
that's all that they could stutter
I said I'm hit upon the head
and the culprit's in the gutter.

You mean to say in all this black
a rocket fell from out the sky.
good job you were not looking up,
it could have been a 'Harold' in the eye.

What chances are of such a happening
am I not of accident prone
let's get that head a looking at,
get walking, let's get home.

George E. Valler

A cold tap and a sodden towel
now sits nursing on my head,
and a family grin from ear to ear
as they all went off to bed.

Sat here in Australia instead of my usual desk at home, I pondered on my writing and what to write about. Then I thought of writing a factual poem instead of fiction. So, although the mishap that I endured was several years ago, I'm still amazed at how it happened and it is still a topic of conversation at some family gatherings.

So, if by a million to one chance you are reading my verse, may I say many a thank you. Fact can be stranger than fiction. If some of you were expecting me to say that we saw Guy Fawkes standing on the footbridge with a barrel of gunpowder, that wouldn't be fact would it - no, no!

CHAPTER 2

As you have gathered by now, I used to live in a village, population not so many, which had a grocer's shop, a tiny bakery run by a robust gent who produced some of the most delicious flaky pastry steak and kidney pies, amongst many other delights.

We also had a blacksmith, yes a blacksmith, old and agile, whose picture and a mention appeared in the local paper of him shoeing a horse at the age of 80 years. Now long gone, my second poem is, I give you - The Smithy.

The Smithy

How loud sings out the hammer
to the anvil's ringing song.
How hot now is the metal
that bends the twisted prong.

The breath of the furnace bellows
turns the grey coals into red.
While glowing are the embers
that light the smithy shed.

A cart stands long forgotten
amid nature's growing shroud.
A horse no longer standing
'neath the gathering of the cloud.

George E. Valler

The smithy with his furnace
sweat deep upon his brow.
His hammer and his strong arm
no longer needed now.

The winds of change as ever
await the modern age.
And history must once again
turn yet another page.

How loud sings out the hammer
to the anvil's ringing song.
How long now is the memory
of an old, old smithy gone.

In my mid-years I started and ran a small business from the house garage. But my good lady and I progressed, employed others and took over a small factory unit. With the children growing up, we began to plan our holidays in the more far-flung places and for some two weeks of the year the factory girls would run the works whilst we went away.

On this occasion, over 20 years plus now, we booked Thailand and joined up with a small group we met up with in Thailand, travelling to tourist places.

One such place, a tour of the infamous Hell Fire Pass and the Bridge on the River Kwai. Built by hand, thousands of soldiers and civilians with hammer and chisel and continuous Japanese guard abuse, hacked their way through solid rock to allow the Thai-Burma Railway to be built through the notorious Burma jungle. Young

Australian, New Zealand and British soldiers and many others, enduring starvation, blistering sun, day and night working and countless flies. It is said that for every railway sleeper laid a life was lost. Do you remember Alec Guinness and the film The Bridge on the River Kwai?

So moved was I by the experience that I wrote the poem which featured in a local radio programme on Anzac Day, where I had the privilege of reading it out - Too Young

Too Young

We were born too young, too young for life
To suffer the edge of the sword and the knife
We were blessed with our youth too young to die
We were born too young for the damned River Kwai.

We were born too young for the hammer and nail
The crack of the whip, the sting of the flail
A hell that was burning from a sun bleached sky
We were born too young for the damned River Kwai.

We were born too young for the rock and the soil
Day turned to night for such senseless toil
The questions we asked, for no reason why
We were born too young for the damned River Kwai.

We were born too young for the cry and the wail
The struggle to lift the limbs that are frail
Not for us is there time or tear left to cry
We were born too young for the damned River Kwai.

George E. Valler

We were born too young for the rail that we lay
The time and the place is the price we all pay
The sweat and the pain, the bite of the fly
We were born too young for the damned River Kwai.

We were born too young for the hands that have bled
We no longer remember the words that were said
Released from our bondage in the earth where we lie
We were born too young for the damned River Kwai.

We were born too young, oh remember us now
Not for us was there time to furrow and plough
We were born too young, too young to die
We were all too young for the damn River Kwai.

CHAPTER 3

In the previous chapter I mentioned the group we met up with in Thailand. There were twelve of us who lived in different parts of the country and decided that it would be good to meet up once a year at different locations where each of us lived. We would spend a couple of days together and afterwards it became a ritual that I would write a poem about the activities we did over our stay. That, together with the odd poem throughout the years was the extent of my poetic writing.

Exactly when I began to take on the more serious side of poetic writing - it had to be during Covid.

It was the pandemic and Facebook that really set the pen and the imagination flowing.

Silent Streets

There's a silence walking down our street,
by day and then by night
while descending down upon us all
the Corona Virus blight.

With liberty now taken
to add to our trouble and strife,
this virus in its vicious form
will even take your life.

George E. Valler

But fate has dealt another hand
by those of us much wiser.
A vaccine now to make the stand
A vaccine needled out by Pfizer.

Whilst the purists in the poetry world will give you reasons on how you should produce poetry, I am of the school of, write what you feel. Your mind has given you the picture - now go and paint it. Most of my poems, and no doubt other poets as we like to call ourselves, come from those flash moments or a situation, for example, my good lady stood at the mirror creating her masterpiece, hence I wrote four poems on the mirror theme. This is one of them.

A Mirror Image

Is this the image as I peek
This mirror image I now seek
The sparkling eyes that outward shine
The skin so smooth without a line
The radiance of a smile caress
The silken hair, have I been blessed
This portrait paint now all to see
So tells the world, yes, this is me
The painting brush so many ways
Lips now smile, the crimson glaze
The twist, the look, yes this is me
This reflected picture now I see
The loveliness I now portray
I really don't know what to say.
But think of all that I've achieved

This picture painted to deceive
Well, no one really needs to know
Just what this canvas doesn't show.

Other poem-triggers come. I may be talking and a few words are said that sets one off, and out pours another verse. For example, I was watching a programme on Oscar Wilde and his story of The Portrait of Dorian Gray, a picture in the attic. At the completion I rushed into my study, although late, and in a very short time - A Mirror in the Attic.

The Mirror in the Attic

I have a mirror painted Dorian
In the attic in my roof
It shows my reflected passing
It shows my passing youth.

Whilst a Dorian painted picture
Never changed from day to day
My mirrored picture image
Shows an age each time I walk away.

He had his picture painted
To retain his young in look
His lifetime in a story
His lifetime in a book.

The picture-painted Dorian
He needed it to stay
His youth retained for always
Not wanting to grow old and grey.

George E. Valler

But my own mirror painted lifetime
My image, my living proof
Each time that I look in
It's a reflection of the truth.

Not then a Dorian image
Let my mirror hold me now
For life is one long spillage
The reflection shows me how.

The picture, a fleeting moment,
Shaded, it is the mirror's loss
I travel across the pictured torment
I am captured within the loft.

My reflection is the street I walk
An image my daily task
For the showing of myself
Not my being just a mask.

If a painted picture I would remain
Not a change as each would say
A mirror image moved and gone
Lost to another day.

So Dorian, must I then grow old
Grow old, forever grey
No painting hidden in the loft
A portrait of a Dorian Gray.

Talking of attics, another poem that came to mind. We use the attic as a forgotten store room. An uncle of my wife recently passed away, and his house now alone, has a loft taped up and not visited for many a year.

The Loft

In our loft there sits in idleness
all the bric-a-brac of the day
the collective needs of nothingness
saved for a rainy day.
Dust now hides the memories
stored in days now long ago
lost, who knows, all wrapped in rows
the loft do we bestow.
Saved now the joys and broken toys
a teddy's one-eyed look
and stories told, pages unfold
like chapters in a book.
A lowly bulb in solitude
hangs a dawning from the dark
and shadows cast their long lost form
to the silence in the stark.
No better place to hide away
out of sight, now out of mind
all our days of yesterday
now left far behind.
In our loft there sits in idleness
all the bric-a-brac in the way
the collective needs of nothingness
saved for a rainy day.

CHAPTER 4

Do you know, whilst writing this little adventure, I found that I could let the poems dictate the journey. So let's do that.

Care Homes, Old Age, Times Past, Aches and Pains, well they are able to offer poetic exploration. So let's go down that road.

Growing Old

The bag of hope, the flowers sweet,
the stick my crutch to bear
but hand in hand you by my side
I have no need to care.

Let's walk the timeless road to nowhere
though our steps they may be slow
for walking life its zebra path
without a map to show.

When you're getting older life tends to find new problems. My mother-in-law had a stroke, and like so many of old age years, she could no longer cope and needed continuous care. Whilst visiting, I was prompted to write - Age and Time

George E. Valler

Age and Time

She gently walks on tender feet
and shuffles through the door
whilst rich in life's past memories
in health she is quite poor.

Her world just seems a smaller place
each step shortened by the day
comfort in the pills she takes
to keep the pain at bay.

So slowly now the chair she sits
relief creased upon her face
days long remembered with a sigh
how life she would embrace.

Time has tolled the living bell
the years have all rolled by
youth no longer in her hands
aged, far too old to try.

But life still has its gentleness
each day a new begin
from window, soft, the sunlight shines
to bright the room within.

A buzzing fly, how nature sounds
encircles now the room
while roses in a crystal vase
smile colours in their bloom.

Safely now the chair she rests
to take away her day
and ponder thus on moments past
while memories fade away.
She gently walks on tender feet
as she has done before
while rich in life's long days now gone
now silence closes the door.

So, with age we have to suffer, for we are visited by our aches and pains.

Mortal Me

If only I could stand without
pain climbing through my knees.
If my ears no longer listen
to the buzzing of the bees.

The back no longer bending,
shoulders no longer take the strain.
The stretching of each muscle
as it argues with the pain.

The steps that once we took before
now shortened by the day.
There's an age that wants to tell us
time no longer wants to play.

The eyes that once all seeing
now grapple with the page.

George E. Valler

All that we could ever do
passed with the coming of the age.

The smiles have stopped their chattering
as they lay drowning in a glass.
So now the time that's played out
puts us out to grass.

Our journey needs an ending
now our journey's nearly done.
How wishful is the thinking
of the days when we were young.

So as we reflect on times past, maybe wishing to be young again,
maybe now there is a different, gentler path.

The Book of Life

The Book of Life sits on the shelf
Charted memories almost gone
For all those forgotten years
Life must surely now move on.

Those joyful moments life caressed
Together was the way
Life so full of hope and joy
We took our chance we had our day.

Oh how we danced, so young back then
Each joyous moment to behold
And with each carefree, spent,

My Life in The Poetry Lane

Our life we let unfold.

Now though still a togetherness
The cup of life is growing cold
For all those passion moment's had
Could now we be growing old.

So now we take a different stand
A more gentle distance kept
No longer now the passion flares
It's time we must accept.

Let's now take a different path
More in keeping with our age
With now all those moments passed
Could life turn another page.

The journeyed road, another mile
The gentle passion now accept
Let the moments now to smile
Look back with no regret.

For of all good fortune told
Passed by those years we cared
Our gentleness in moments now
No better life could we have shared.

CHAPTER 5

In the mid-seventies when we moved into our village, just a few miles out of town, this was our very first real home. Three up, three down, bathroom, garage, garden. To my good lady and me it was heaven, our own little palace, and me being me, decided on a few changes. You know, extend the room downstairs, fit central heating, open up a wall - all by my own hand. Then one day it will all be a memory. My little poem on memory lane will do nicely here.

Memory Lane

Take down the windows of memory
let life bounce around the walls
explore the steps of memory
down the passageway of halls.

Let the joys of life swing open
swing open memories door
and sweep the pain and suffering
from off the memory floor.

The recipes of pleasure
hot off the memory grate
stack away in memories cupboard
among the memories and the plates.

George E. Valler

Let the basement hold dark memories
down the dark and distant past
In the parlour hang the memories
In pictured, memories to last.

Now you have your bricks and mortar
of the memories you call home
now the memories of the future
are the roads that you must roam.

The one thing I am finding, that the poems telling the story can be quite random. But it does make for a more interesting read, don't you think, and poets seem to dwell on love so I ask the question

Love is Just a Word

Am I not of good fortune bent
When life to me my sweet wife lent.
Did she from heaven of that I'm sure
She made life rich, saved me from poor.
She opened life's Aladdin's Cave
Reminded, days are heaven paved.
Is she the sun that lights the day
And chased the devils far away.
Without could not life be the same
Is she the sun, is she the rain.
This flowered garden, beauty is mine
The seasons show now every time.
The stars that read my fortunes way
Remind me each and every day.
Then, am I of good fortune bent

When life to me my good wife sent.

Whilst on this nostalgic journey let's include this poem I rather like. It's got nothing to do with the village but I rather liked it. It's called The Winding Path

The Winding Path

Take me down the winding path
to where the weeping willows cry
where bluebells ring their chorus line
to a dawning bright blue sky.

Let me listen to the woodland pipes
as the lark pirouettes on the wing
the forest rests its weary limbs
as the breeze now gently sings.

See the wild rose, all is smiling
the primrose her yellow hue
the woodland creatures stirring
amid the early morning dew.

It's the sight and sound of the woodland
that makes me ponder for a while
it's the winding path to nowhere
lays upon me that gentle smile.

As you know when we moved into our first house, we did some changes. This poem then will relate to not just me, but to many of you. How often have you moved house, the great trauma of your

George E. Valler

life, then what do you do? We had some friends who seemed to be always on the move and since Mr. Husband was a very useful D.I.Y.er I wrote this simple little tongue-in-cheek poem, with the question - why are we building a house on the side!

Building a House on the Side

We're building a house on the side
for this one is not very wide
and oh didn't I mention
we wanted an extension.
So we're building a house on the side

Our last house was so very nice
we really had to think twice
but we've downsized you see
and it's really not me.
Now we're building a house on the side.

The scaffolding's up all around
and we've dug all the holes in the ground
we've bought tiles for the floor
and there's concrete to pour.
For we're building a house on the side.

The architect who drew up the plans
is counting the rooms on his hands
while the builder without feeling
wants to knock down the ceiling.
Cause we're building a house on the side.

My Life in The Poetry Lane

We've plasterers and plumbers galore,
and tilers who've been here before,
we've a jack-of-all-trades
for we're having things made.
As we're building a house on the side.

With windows and doors now all in
and even a new wheelie bin,
I've noticed I'm sure,
It's as big as before.
Why are we building a house on the side!

CHAPTER 6

Shall we consider children on our poetic journey and write for them in a more light-hearted vein.

The Wasp

The wasp he can sting many times
in stinging he is quite free
but nature in her wisdom
gave just one sting to the bee.
While the bee is oh so busy
building up her hive
the wasp in his wily solitude
seems looking for more ways to skive.
He'll come dashing through the flowers
he doesn't give a damn
when it comes to easy pickings
he'll come looking for your jam.
With his flashy yellow waistcoat
and his stinging yellow tail
he feels he's God's creation
a type we all know well.
But it's the window that seems to get him
he seems to have lost the plot
for a newspaper rolled, in a hand,
leaves him just a yellow striped splot!!

George E. Valler

Do you remember the poem by Mary Howitt, The Spider and the Fly. This is my version.

The Spider

'Come into my parlour said the spider to the fly'

We can talk about the weather
while the sun scorches through the sky
I can spin you yarns about my web
you can tell me how you fly.

While you a humble fly may be
the world's there at your feet
you can dash around the sky
you can fly down every street.

But life can be so lonely
as I sit here all alone
when darkness descends around me
and the wind just wants to moan.

So fly, come then, tell me
of places that you roam
and are there others like you
do you really have a home.

Tell me about old waspy
he seems a nasty type
throwing all his weight around
creating all that hype.

Now take the bee she is more humble
As she gets on building a home
travelling her flowered world
to find the sweetness, she must roam.

Well, come into my parlour
take the weight then off your feet
for it must be awfully tiring
dashing up and down those streets.

But spider, come into your parlour?
I have to ask the question - why?
for to come into your parlour
You are a spider, me a fly!

The Fly

I've called him Rupert
I don't know why
Because after all
He's only a fly.

But he can climb windows
Fly up to the sky
Can I do that?
Oh no, not I.

So I watch as he dances
around in the air
and wonder what he thinks
or does he really care

George E. Valler

He's too small to bother
with life's worrying tests
he can just be a nuisance
very annoying at best.

But a fly has a lifespan
quite short you can see
because Rupert in his wisdom
is now annoying me.

A child's world is not always happy and carefree. Remembering there is the more sorrowful side. I apologise in advance for possibly making you feel sad, but this is unfortunately life's reality and I wrote it because I could not think of a more lonely existence than that of the forgotten child.

The Forgotten Child

The door is locked and bolted
as I sit here in my room.
My head it is still hurting
where mummy hit me with a broom.

I wish I wasn't so hungry
after all I've had my slice of bread.
But that was really yesterday
when I was sent to bed.

The floor is hard beneath my blanket
there's no pillow for my head.
So I'm sitting in the corner
with my arms around my legs.

My Life in The Poetry Lane

The sun shines through the windows
I watch dust dancing in its rays.
A fly buzzes all around the room
Spinning round as in a daze.

Daddy left a sausage yesterday
it seemed an awful sin.
But mummy said 'you've had enough'
and threw it in the bin.

My head again is hurting
for I can feel the bruise.
The room moves all around me
and leaves me so confused.

The door is locked and bolted
and I'm in here to stay.
I wish I was just like a bird
then I could fly away.

I'd fly up to a fairyland
with cakes and sweets galore.
And have a great big comfy bed
not sleep upon the floor.

I'd give some cake to mummy
daddy, too, there's some for him.
Perhaps I could have that sausage
that was thrown down in the bin.

George E. Valler

I try to love my mummy
and my daddy too.
But they don't seem to want to know
so what more then can I do.

I think I'll close my eyes now
and try so hard to pray.
I've already had my slice of bread
but that was yesterday.

May I end this children's chapter on a reflective note.

It was whilst watching my grandson open his Christmas presents that he took the biggest box, and while ignoring his thoughtfully purchased gifts, he proceeded to climb into the box and play all afternoon, making up different scenarios for himself and the box.

It's the inspiration of a box that says so many things - a blank canvass to the future.

The Box

I had a box last night
it was big and brown
with a crumpled side
in which my world could fit inside
I had a box last night.

I had a box last night
in which I travelled near and far
I saw a moon I saw a star

My Life in The Poetry Lane

as I travelled in my crumpled car
I had a box last night.

I had a box last night
I sang a song upon the sea
the song I sang was after tea
in my crumpled boat I made for me
I had a box last night.

I had a box last night
where I rode the range on a coal black steed
chasing cows at break neck speed
counting all the steers I'd got
 hidden in my crumpled box
I had a box last night.

I had a box last night
in which I hid when dragons roared
and put to flight with flashing sword
In my crumpled castle made of board
I had a box last night.

I had a box last night
in which I lay to rest my head
with Mr. Sandman overhead
Asleep, asleep in my crumpled bed
I had a box last night.

Alas today my box must go
No stage to set no life to show
for mummy says it cannot stay
and really must be thrown away

George E. Valler

It clutters up the box it seems
where mummy sits with all her dreams.

I had a box last night.

CHAPTER 7

Poets are known for lamenting on their lost love, precious love or forever love. I also have a loving pen and desire.

She Danced So Light

She danced so light on pretty feet
held out her arms for us to meet.
Around and round our lives revolved
tripping light, all problems solved.
She is the dawn upon my day
she is the wind that moments sway.
The sun that shines in golden glow
how much my love she'll never know.
Her innocence in eyes that shine
she is forever, always mine.
This little lady of the night
give to my eyes, my eyes delight.
So with form and shape one cannot say
yet turns that night back into day.
So dance she light on pretty feet
now time will chance forever meet.

When I really got into writing poems I looked up a poetry publisher (as you do of course); one publisher had a category where a picture was shown and you the budding poet were to write your poetic version - this is called Ekphrastic Poetry, a poem describing a scene

George E. Valler

or work of art. The picture showed a loose dog, people, some in the foreground and some in the background, walking down a dowdy, hot sunny street. There you have the scene, now write!

The Street,

They walk the street by light of day
and shout the dog that's in their way.
His sniffing nose their ankles check
and would take bite if they would let.

But come behind another soul
to pass this way as if in stroll.
Whilst those gone forward, already passed,
have no need take him to task.

The road ahead, sun-drenched and bare,
never he, who wants to share.
A challenge from across the road
reminds them this is his abode.

Who guards this stretch with snarl and tooth
he does not care for their reproof.
The distance kept might well remind
of those that stroll from far behind.

He is the master of this race
looked on, as always, with distaste.
They take his street as if their right
Would not they risk if it were night.

Tread light your foot on silent limb
could well you come across of him.
For lurk is he, of hide he seeks,
so corner is upon his street.

Take life, take yours, keep it in hand
a journey needs, a journey planned.
Street, upon your footfalls walk
continue, constant prowling stalk.

Domain is his, he is the Street,
he keeps it guard, there's no retreat.
Must then he growl and bark all day.
Would you not want of him to play.

While we say that poets are ten a penny, it's fortunate to have the ability to write a good verse, paint a picture for the reader. A poem just for you.

Come to think of it, this poetic writing of mine began, as stated before, at the start of the pandemic.

We were on holiday in Australia, early 2020, staying with our daughter. We were panicking because flights were being cancelled and toilet rolls were being fought over in Aussie supermarkets.

Our flight was one of the last to leave. My poem for the moment was.

George E. Valler

Aboard the A380

We climbed aboard the A380 with bags stowed in the hold
feeling rather smug because we hadn't caught a 'cold'.
Australia we are leaving, dashing back to the old UK
pursued by Corona Virus, that cut short many a tourist stay.
The seats are rather narrow as we sat down in our place
but the fellow sitting next to me had a smile upon his face.
The aircraft was filling up, filling up right to the brim,
the journey ever onward was looking rather grim.
He looked across and winked at me, not sure what he had in mind
I thought perhaps just friendly, thought perhaps just being kind.
But, then he leaned ever closer and with an old Australian drawl
from out beneath his coat he pulled a brand new toilet roll.
Would I just like to buy it, it's quite rare I'm sure
but it was going to leave me penniless, leave me rather poor.
Don't worry about that he said, it's a present from the past.
You will then remember this moment, whenever you wipe your ****

Talking of holidays and foreign lands, the other side of life is brought home to you.

I remember when we were holidaying in Jamaica. You get to know the staff around. One young lad was desperate for me to give him my trainers when I left. Some years later I wrote.

My Left Foot

Please sir may I have a shoe
I know I shouldn't ask

for barefoot I rough and tumbled
through the dirt tracks of my past.
You may feel one shoe only
is such a strange request
for one seems so odd at least
but I do not need any less.
I've never had a pair of shoes
I've got along quite well
but as time and life rolled on
my needs began to tell.
More important were the other things,
a head above water so to speak
for I was told that what I sow
will repay in what I reap.
But nature in her wisdom
decided to play another trick
so now you see in my hand
a wooden walking stick.
So please could you spare a shoe
I know I shouldn't ask
It need not be a new one
even an old off-cast.
For I know it's going to help me
my one foot in a shoe
my other lost, forgotten,
that's why I've come to you.

A few years ago I decided to take the family on holiday to the island of Minorca. Looking forward with everything prepared, a letter dropped through the letterbox saying that we needed to change our holiday as the travel company could not fulfil their obligations.

George E. Valler

So we chose Lindos on the island of Rhodes, which was beautiful. We were lucky to choose an alternative, others had not been so fortunate.

The Five Letter Word

We've chosen our holiday we're going abroad,
now they've sent us a five letter word.

We've filled in the booking self catering with cooking,
and two rooms with a possible third.

We wanted Phuket but the place was all let,
so they offered me Botany Bay.

I said that's absurd it's a place I've not heard,
I'd rather have Malta in May.

Well that's the trouble we must burst your bubble,
wrote the start of that five letter word.

Now I fear it's no joke the company's gone broke,
and BROKE is the five letter word!

CHAPTER 8

As we open up Chapter 8 and looking out of the window, the clouds are rolling in, there is a promise of rain and heavy cloud as evening draws to night.

I Am Moon

Reach out to me you bubbling clouds
I am the light of night
I am the baying echo call
of nature's rapturous light
I keep the season's earthly call
I keep the stars aglow
I am the romance there for all
my golden light to show
Reach out to me you bubbling clouds
let's shake a golden hand
my moonlight vision to behold
across the darkened land.

Time would you say for coffee? While coffee is the popular drink, and how many shades can you have? I rather like the cup that helped the war, a good old cup of tea.

That brings to mind an old tradition, the reading of the tealeaves. Do you remember?

George E. Valler

Tea Leaves and Me

I read my tea leaves yesterday
now I must take stock
It read 'my favourite colour - pink'
It gave me quite a shock.
My masculinity now in question
my hand stroking my beard
I stood alone and shaking
feeling really rather weird.
I know I poured the water hot
the leaves I stirred around
but there is no need to question
I know my gender's sound.
Was it because I used Darjeeling
instead of that Yorkshire brew
the sort that claims it's masculinity
maybe it helps your nether regions too.
But wait, let's look into the mirror
just give me time to think
after all it fits quite well, this dress.
resplendent all in pink.

How often we poets exchange ideas and comments on each other's work. You correspond by the printed word but may never have met the person directly. It came to me that you get to know someone whilst out of sight, you see them only as print. So I wrote - The Printed Face

The Printed Face

I know I have never met you
I've not seen you face to face
you've been only a sentence
with a full stop in its place.
To me you've been a chapter
a chapter and a verse
I've never had to shake your hand
wish for better or for worse.
I see you as in rhyming form
each line a new remind
words that forward tell the day
and never leave behind.
You are those timeless moments
that stretch across the page
timeless are the moments
words that will never age.
You are you see the question mark
the answer and full stop
you are the rubbing out mistake
the lost word now forgot.
I see you as the pen that writes
a sentence twisted and mistook
you are, of course, the written word
each chapter in a book.

It is quite surprising how odd little situations crop up and leaves you thinking - have you ever noticed how people, some are boisterous all over the place, some form groups and odd ones are left on the periphery of life. Some people are Wallflowers.

George E. Valler

Don't Hide Little Wallflower

Don't hide among the bushes
one day the leaves will fall.
Just climb up through the branches
to make yourself feel tall.
For life can be a blessing
as well as a blessed curse.
By climbing tall before the fall
you're way above the worst.
Just embrace the joy of living
this miracle that is you.
Just remember who you are
you're a million among the few.
Time may rest upon your shoulders
your hopes may seem to pass you by.
Let not 'hide' then be your shelter
you no longer need be shy.
The world can be your every day
to stand out among the crowd.
You have no need to hide away
being you, you're being proud.
Don't hide among the bushes
just rise above it all.
Don't hide among the bushes
one day the leaves will fall.

Yes, all the leaves will fall, especially when this happens.

Cold, Cold the Day

Cold snaps the welcome frost glazed day
Shimmering paths now mark the way
Forest leaves like silver tongues
Reach out with joy the breaking sun
Where waters bled ice crystals hang
Froze through the night like sharp wolf fang
Carpet white spread hill and dell
While distant rings the tolling bell
A robin, nature's winter life
Flits branch to branch through winter's knife
Reflected puddles, iced mirrors speak
A palace, crystal garden bleak
So come the sun to melt the day
Oh pictured frost now pass away
We now have seen oh nature, stay
Let tomorrow freeze another day.

CHAPTER 9

I often wondered when writing my poems (I like to call them verse) at what stage would you be able to call yourself a poet. It seems a few lines of verse and suddenly everyone's a poet. So I ask the question.

Call Yourself a Poet

Dear colleagues, may I ask of you a question
although I won't take you to task.
It's a question that's had me thinking
it's a question I now wish to ask.

If I wrote a few words as a sonnet
paint a picture, use an old scratchy pen.
Should I consider, then, myself a poet
give myself a mark, a mark, perhaps out of ten.

I know I'm just Mr. Ordinary
I'm not a Shelley or a Blake.
I'll not sit at the poetic table
nor take a slice of the poetry cake.

If I was an architect or a lawyer
or a teacher who knew the score.
I would need years of time and study

George E. Valler

before my claim to open that door.

Perhaps if I tore down the start of creation
ripped up the rivers of life.
Created both hell and damnation
painted pictures of trouble and strife.

Find words in my palette of colour
see the blue in the heavens above.
Write words we now take for granted
of feelings, of thought and of love.

Perhaps when I have moulded my writing
crafted skills that remember the past.
Put memories down upon paper
verse that I know then will last.

To open life's fleeting moments
reach out to open that door.
So my words they are read and spoken
those words that are now needed more.

Will I scatter life's seeds all around
seeds of life, that's how I will show it.
Only then will I earn the words that I yearn
yes, can I now have the title - A Poet.

I don't know about you, but in our house I'm the one who makes the early morning coffee. It all began with a morning moment, who makes the first drink of the day?

One of the joys in life, my wife maintains, is just that. The nectar of the morning rise, but who makes the first cup. Well it has been democratically agreed that we take it in turns, like a work pattern one day on, one day off. The days on became the norm for me! (I walk the stairs each day at dawn) - keeps me young I am told as we have a three storey house!!

Morning Call

The early morning rises
with sleep still in my head.
The sheet and softness pillows
no longer pull me back to bed.
The flushing of the toilet bowl
with water in the sink.
And windows open wide
clear my mind with time to think.
The stairs, each tread is calling,
step into the dawning new.
The doors of life swing open
to inhale the grassy dew.
For Mondays, Wednesdays, Fridays,
I am awakened to the call.
To take my weary steps downstairs
and then across the hall.
To pull out the cups and saucers
from the cupboard way on high.
The kettle, like a sentry,
like a sentry standing by.
Soon it will be boiling
steam curling like a snake.
For a welcome cup this morning

well, that's what I intend to make.
So, what's it all about then
this early morning call.
Well, it's just a grand awakening
a welcome for us all.

And of course the morning has to awake, so a nice little verse on the morning rise.

This Early Jewel

It's the dawn that rolls the morning sky
and calls awake both you and I.
The pillow talk, enough now said
need now to step, walk from the bed.
So claim awake the daylight hour
a moment's take to now devour.
Night hides not, for all too soon,
dark now calls, now calls the moon.

Many years ago before I started my own business, a friend of mine asked me to join him. He had at this time started a new venture. One of the perks of the offer was a car. However, when I was not using the car he would make use of it himself. On one occasion when he and I had been out long hours working, we came back to the office and I, to pick up my car late at night. My journey home was through a lonely forest area. The car stopped (out of petrol) - I had not been warned, hence my lonely dark night-walk. Accompanied by the odd owl hoot.

As I Walk

As I walk the road before
as I step the tarmac black
as I stride the houses pass
so shine the lights above the stack
as I walk the pavement night
I walk the shine therein the light
so shall the threat that promise rain
as I walk the steps forward gain
so shall the doors the windows shut
I walk the light the shadows cut
so shall my journey take me forth
do I walk both south or north
so shall I step the forward stride
have I not, no not, to hide
so shall the call, the owl, her flight
so shall she see in dark of night
on silent wing her bounty all
so shall I not hear then her call
oh hear then I the bark of dog
so shall I now this highway slog
the dawn, the dawn, the break of day
so I walk my weary way.

I think it's nice to have a poem that can convey a certain amount of humour. Cycling has now developed a club following. That gave me a thought. While the lads are on their bikes, well how about......

George E. Valler

The Bike

We've been married quite some time
well in years it seems a lot
but now he seems to have lost interest
lost interest in - well - you know what!

He spends all hours in his shed
and me I sit alone in bed.

He's into blasted cycling
lycra - he's bought the lot.
I think he'd rather ride his bike
than with me and - you know what!

When I look into the mirror
as life turns another page
I must admit I don't look bad
not bad now for my age.

Perhaps I ought to look around
around to see what's what
and maybe find that something else
maybe I might - well - you know what!

I remember when at first we met
to the bedroom we would trot
to do the things you do in bed
you know, in bed - well - you know what!

Now all the time he's with that bike
in that blasted shed
Instead of - well - you know what!
With me and us in bed.

But last night he burst into the room
in that manly excited way
and took me into his arms
he had something to say.

He held me tight and close
in that good old fashioned manner
and said 'Luv I need you now -
can you come and hold me spanner'!!

While we are on the subject of cycling on the proverbial bike.

The Ballad of the Cyclist

The peddled feet doth haul the chain
through weather all come shine come rain.
Rubber wheels do tarmac track
and ride must show a Day-Glo mac.
Saddle high, firm feet do press,
tradition, lycra, the cyclist dress.
So many a gear to ease my plight
swift onward roll in forward flight.
So hill, so dale, so tough terrain
I think next time I'll go by train.

CHAPTER 10

Sometimes a moment comes to me while I am in conversation. I put it down on paper in an instant. Talking to one of my poetry friends on paper and reading one of his rather raunchy renditions, before I knew it I had written my own reply.

LUST

As I look at her, lust in my eye
She turns and says, don't even try
You are long past your sell by date
All of that is far too late.

Those longings that you had before
Are now at last a closing door
All those days when you were young
That tension spring is now well sprung.

Now that you are in your dotage
Let life turn another page
And if all that is not enough
Then damn well act your age.

Now that we are on that subject, how about a little tongue in cheek poem, written a little bit differently, an alternate view.

George E. Valler

Can We Have Sex Again

Can we have sex again
sex again, that's what he said
can we have sex again,
as we sat up there in bed

But you have already had it
you had it last July
and as for having it again
you can kiss that thought goodbye

You can be so demanding
wanting to have it once again
soon you will be wanting
wanting then to use a cane

Just then the lodger knocked our door
upon our door! while we're in bed!
then, while slowly opening it
you won't believe just what he said

Can we have sex again, sex again
I could not believe my ears
my husband turned and looked at me
in his eyes I could see the tears

He jumped right out of bed
what he would do I'm not quite sure
but he went over and took his hand
and they both walked out the door.

Well let's move on. This poem was written as an Ekphrastic entrant to a competition (a poem based on a picture). This was a picture of a weather-beaten billboard, the torn paper adverts in various states of degradation. Lost underneath the layers of other adverts was now exposed a picture of a very sweet girl advertising some product, my poem a little deeper than my normal style - I give you

Picture Billboard Me

Tear down my youth as you can see
am I not young as all of me.
My picture aged, but I am young
still smile the pleasure I must view.
Tear down this young, this young is me
but old perhaps, tear tells a tale.
Of youth I was, as youth still am
weathered torn as now no longer.
Gone my vision need no more
I am of yesterday, yet look today.
Am I not still this vision young
with edges torn as weathered, aged.
Covered, tried as if to hide of me
no longer need for all to see.
Some tried blotting image new
no message could compete.
I am of ageless, ageing time
yet sweet the innocence I show.
No cover could strip my picture
leave me torn, stripped but whole.
I am of innocence portrayed, sweet me,
yesterday I was, today still am.

George E. Valler

Most poets, in fact I would say the majority, like writing about love, that little word, the whole world seems to turn on - so, another Ekphrastic poem, based on a picture of love letters hidden within the branches of a tree.

Love Letters

Beneath this tree a hallowed ground
where once together love we found.
When spring uplifting, grass would grow
so feelings we as both could show.

The tenderness of touch we feel
as summer turns its spinning wheel.
Those little notes in secret wrote
watch tender leaves as breeze did stroke.

Each day we came like summer's thrill
lay watch the clouds above them spill.
The branches swaying, lovers' dream
another note thus penned a theme.

Now winter claws its frost-like hand
to hide the notes in twisted band.
Hidden hope within the tree
now stares awake for all to see.

Beneath this tree this hallowed ground
where once together love we found.
Now memories such as we have lost
tied in a band in winters frost.

My Life in The Poetry Lane

Love between two people has not always been easy

Beauty and the Night

Oh how I wish to kiss
that suntanned face
those golden lips
I wish to taste
to feel your form
upon my chest
your body shape
'neath cotton dress
those golden hands
fingers entwined
those almond eyes
I wish were mine
that smile so sweet
upon your face
such feelings show
that you embrace
no choice, but we
must surely part
for I am light
and you are dark

Life is such a mystery, questions on why are we here, what is our meaning, is there a God, who could the Devil really be. I have written one or two poems on the Grim Reaper and old Lucifer

George E. Valler

The Reaper

Had the Reaper visit today
he called just passing through
he spoke a voice I couldn't hear
I said, I didn't think that I was due

As he floated in his faceless shroud
his scythe held shoulder high
I've come here to save you all
when you wish this world goodbye

I am the people's gardener
I prune the withered from their beds
I save them from their misery
from this life that they have led

I thought, I'll come and show you
the place where you could dwell
where you can have your wishes
don't ask why they call it Hell

I can also show you Heaven,
show you that Heaven in the sky
but whether anyone is there
can't say, but we can try

Our place can be warm and cosy
a really nice place to dwell
and with your worldly mates down here
you'll settle in quite well

My Life in The Poetry Lane

I thanked him for his thoughtfulness
but said I'm not ready yet
but when I am, should I call
it means you don't have to fret

He climbed aboard his Reaper's cart
shovelled on a lump of coal
and as he disappeared from sight
I thought 'my what a friendly soul'

CHAPTER 11

I wrote a poem once about a moth just a few lines, sort of abstract. They say poetry can have a meaning even when 'way-out'. I was once in conversation with a poetry editor who sent me some 'way-out' poetry and told me to read it through and try to understand what the poet had in mind. So here is the moth poem 'what I wrote' (to quote Ernie Wise) and I will follow on with my interpretation of a possible meaning.

THE MOTH

The rusted bar hangs 'neath a shedless roof
the moth, perched, landed, unspoken,
uninvited upon, hangs legless
caught in its mind the hope
spread light the sun as beats the rod
moth hounded, need for mind to speak
die death, last speaks the mothless breath
and die, shrivelled sun-drenched dry,
a rusted mothless hollow shell.

The following is my interpretation of the subconscious possible meaning.

The shed is the world, a roofless ruin; the rusted bar, a precarious hold on life; the sun, global warming beating down relentlessly; the moth is life, frail, vulnerable, legless, lost in its hold on life, the inevitable, to fall, to die, to follow the demise of the shed, the road to ruin.

Sadness knocks on everyone's door somewhere along the way and we all have to deal with it. This poem is a little sad because that's how we poets write, poets and sadness seem to go together. Poetry can make a good sad story.

So Tolls the Bell

I will sit by your bedside, dear husband,
The dawn of a new summer morn
I will tell you the world as we know it
Of the days when our children were born
I'll remember when we were together
Your eyes, through the world you would view
Your hands so soft and so gentle
Yet so strong was the work they could do
As you laughed with the children around you
As often you put them to bed
They even now still remember
The stories from the books that you read
How you smiled in that special way
As I angrily stamped on the floor
How you, always the gentleman,
Always there to open a door
When life though seemed against us
And the world just wanting to sway
You held me close in your arms
Tomorrow will be a new day
Do you remember the moment we first met

I can even remember the street
How you held my hand oh so gently
That moment made us complete
Those days long ago our first meeting
Never thinking could it last to this day
But the years have rolled by oh so quickly
Dear Husband, what more can I say
I could tell you the day and the time now
I could even tell you the year
But I know as you lie there sleeping
My voice you no longer hear
May these memories of life stay with us
To us they will always be part
No one could ever replace you
You are forever locked in my heart

And if that is not enough to make you cry in your beer, or tea, or coffee, then when that time is here and you have to say the final goodbye, may I help you with

Weep Not

Do not weep for me tomorrow
as now that I have gone
For tomorrow is the future
and the road will carry on
Just read through all our memories
of the life we had before
Let us walk our days of yesterday
as the closing of the door
Just step into the future

George E. Valler

walk on the days ahead
New memories you will make again
life's moments to be read

The Journey

The pain of grief sits heavy
the special someone no longer there
remember those special moments
you were privileged to share
While the road ahead seems lonely
the darkness stretching long
you can treasure now the memories
that will always keep you strong

Well, after all that, the tears will have played havoc with the makeup, so let's get in front of that mirror and do some paint and brush up, let's just show what we can do, (with a little bit of help)

Mirror Mirror

The mirror loves each powdered brush
As each movement turns to blush
Highlights red and darkened brows
Damned the crows, the cream rebels
Are they not lines come out to play
I wish the Hell they'd go away
I just can't leave what nature's left
As this is now I've been bequest
I seek the image I once knew
A natural picture, oh so true

So mirror mirror on the wall
My daily task to you I call
Make me princess, a princess make
Give it all that I can take
Let Kings proclaim, their hearts do break
But am I not a mirrored fake

The Environment, what a chilling reminder to have on your breakfast plate, but we are constantly reminded that we are on a journey that we need to stop.

The Green Hill

There is a green hill far away
Ravaged by a forest fire
The time is getting desperate
The time is getting dire
The warnings they are with us
No matter where we turn
It's a problem we are facing
To change our ways
To look and learn
So what then of the future
Can anyone really tell
Is this then the beginning
Of the tolling of the bell
Or is it that the green hill
The green hill we seek to know
Could then that very green hill
Let us reap what we must sow

George E. Valler

This little poem will perhaps lift our spirits, for that time of year we call autumn and the question

Autumn

Is it autumn in the time frame
In the time frame of a plant
When the leaves are gently falling
and the earth is softly damp

What tells the tree this time frame
is it temperature or time
Or is it the axe man cometh
to chop down this tree sublime

No, this is mother-nature
as she plans for next year's day
Autumn prepares the sleeping time
before the winter stay

For come the new tomorrow
when spring blossoms in array
This autumn tree shall spread its leaf
to welcome another day

Sometimes one can write a simple verse that has depth that just seems to roll along, just flows rather nicely in its simplicity, yet carries a message. May I open for you

The Door

There is a door, the sign above
'Divorce' just step this way
It has a handle, one each side
there are two sides so they say

For when life's bed of roses
has fallen into decay
all those dedications
now have gone astray

The door is heavy laden
it struggles with such pain
the days of remembered sunshine
now stormy, filled with rain

There is of course the other side
where the journey takes you to
the garden of your memories
will need some digging through

Don't open this door lightly
be sure of all you leave
for once this door is open
it's so hard to retrieve

Just to add to this sorry tale - a reason?

George E. Valler

Forbidden

How sweet forbidden fruit we dine
Forbidden fruit, turned into wine
At lovers' table, stolen time
Drink deep the harvest of our crime
Stay the thought another life
Freedom, away this troubled strife
But stay the thought, another life
Just stay the thought, another wife!

CHAPTER 12

An airport is going to be built at the bottom of your drive. A factory is in planning, outside your back door. Your house is in the way of a new railroad. Welcome to

H S 2

There's a railway coming your way
It's coming crashing through the land
The rails that tear across the fields
Oh yes it's all been planned
No longer will there be
The singing of the lark
The dogs you took for walking
Across those green land parks
The stations and the signals
Announce the coming of the train
The field the farmers ploughing
No longer growing grain
The houses that are in its path
This monster will devour
And when at last it's all complete
They'll be flying by each hour
The speed that we are going
No longer is enough
For these trains to thunder through
It will be two hundred plus
And when these flashing moguls

George E. Valler

All sitting in this train
Will be too busy working
To notice you, out in the rain
It's going to cost us billions
Tear the countryside apart
And despite all the eager protests
It will just go ahead and start
The purse strings they have pulled
From the many for the few
Will you still be standing waiting
For a train that's overdue
While the views across the fields are lost
To those sat working inside
The question you will ask yourself
Was it really worth the ride.

Well after all that, you need to make up your mind, so how about a poem on the mind.

Simple Minds

How vast then is the mind
In this great divide of ours
the mind that is all powerful
this mind and all its powers

A mind to travel infinite
across the universe
to glory us in knowledge
for better or for worse

A mind that turns upside down
a mind to make us think
to make our thoughts so simple
we can record, in pen and ink

A mind to tell where we are going
a mind to tell where we have been
to warn of hidden perils
to tell us how to dream

The stars they may be countless
the mind has counted them before
for no matter where you are
the mind will find an open door

So you ask the mind a question
who am I, a question so profound
the answer's all around you
if you look, then you have found

There is each day a reminder of just how fortunate we are in this old earth. Well she is all we have, she's not a bad soul really. Sure. she kicks back when she feels like it to remind us of her displeasure, but she has a nice side too, she is.

This Earthly Jewel

Dawn lays her head against the sun
as clouds open up the sky
and rain that earlier did fall
now awaits the wind to dry.

George E. Valler

The peace, her silence shattered
by the squawking black eyed crow
the forest in her finery
now looks for time to grow.
Lonely tolls a ringing bell
across the greater plain
where last before the break of dawn
fell plentiful the rain.
Cattle raise their grazing heads
to nature's glorious morn
now heaven shows her faith again
another day is born.

My early childhood days when growing up was surrounded by a world at war. My education was to be given by a reluctant retired old village schoolmaster who tried to manage all of us kids best he could. Sure, we walked to school on our own (no Chelsea tractors then) and come the lunch break we were off into the woods playing Robin Hood.

On one occasion several of us kids decided to roam further afield. Now our old school had a single bell, never used, hung forever in silence in the lofty heights of a tower. When we kids had not returned at the appointed hour the poor old teacher left with a load of his chicks missing took a chance, clever I must say, and tolled the bell into existence. I was the one who on hearing this unexpected sound realised it must be our school bell, and we were missing. Panic, as we all raced back to the classroom. I can't remember any reprimand perhaps the teacher was just glad to have us back safe and sound.

The Learning

I have my education
I know the Earth's no longer flat
An apple and old gravity
Yes I know all about that
I know displacement of a ship
Is equal to its weight
I know that to ask a girl out
You could call it perhaps a date
I know we have cures for most things
Operations injections the like
We have our own N H S
Who are going out on strike
I know tomorrow's always coming
And yesterday has already gone
When it comes to question and answers
You can be right and also wrong
I know that climbing up a hill
Is harder than rolling down
They say that muscles in a smile
Are less than in a frown
I know that if you wait for a bus
There's none and then there's three
I know when you plant a sapling
It will grow into a tree
Now I have my education
There's no longer need to try
I've gathered by life's teachings
All I need to get me by.

George E. Valler

Talking about school and children, they have grandads, we all have, or had, grandads. They play a big part in a youngster's life. This is one of my early poems on a child's eye view of grandad, curious to understand why grandads are just that little bit different.

Grandad

Grandad are you very old
'cause mummy says you are
that's why you wear an overcoat
when riding in the car

And is your hair real silver
and where's the rest all gone
and why do you call that rocking chair
your favourite sit-upon

Grandad are you very old
and were you once a child
'cause mummy gets quite cross with you
she says you drive her wild

And Grandad do you close your eyes
to pretend you are asleep
'cause I've seen you open one a bit
and have a crafty peep

Grandad are you really old
when you talk about the war
and when your eyes are 'resting'
is that why you always snore

Why do grownups when they talk to you
do they have to be so loud
mummy also says you're stubborn
but then sometimes you make her proud

Grandad are you very old
just how am I to tell
when people come around and say
you're looking very well

Oh grandad won't you talk to me
don't close your eyes and sleep
open up, please, just the one
like you do to have a peep

Oh, grandad don't just leave me
with nothing else to say
perhaps I should be quiet
and go off out to play

Grandad are you very old
they say you've had your day
but, grandad, I won't let them
come and take you far away

That was a poem written some time ago when I used to write at odd moments. Now I have a new version. How about grandads, yes we all like to think we are the best. "Look in that mirror son, that's me you're looking at when I was a lad" and the retort "Oh no grandad not another 'when I was a lad' story! Since we have moved on I have called this version.

George E. Valler

Our Little Man

Yes, we called him our little man
as he stumbled through the day
and grandad was his favourite
in each and every way

It was, "grandad will you sit by me"
and "grandad will you hold my hand"
for grandad he was always there
like the sea that washed the sand

But then when five or six, the years,
he now had new demands
it was nana who took over
it was nana who took his hand

And grandad, well now left behind
his hand no longer needed
the sea no longer washed the sand
like a garden no longer weeded

To school, the years expanded
time now was growing up
with books and into learning
to chase life's golden cup

In sport he was to kick about
to go chasing after his dreams
and soon to realise that life
is not always as it seems

On occasions with dear old grandad
a glass or two was rather nice
of course there was a reason
he needed grandad's advice

So now the years have rolled along
time has passed, many would say
and grandads, they are always there
to help along the way.

Now, when he comes to see me
I still call him, our little man,
for when he comes to see me
he's come to hold my hand

As I said earlier in my writing, 'When I was a lad' how often do you get us older generation reminiscing on the good old days, when we walked everywhere, because you had to. How you played outside because indoors was so closed and uninteresting. How you ate berries from the hedgerow, why, because food was in so short supply, an apple was a treat and the war seemed to just go on. Well just think of today's poor souls, what memories will they have to look back on.

Yesterday' Child

Oh remember the days
when we were young
a computer in our hands
sitting in a bedroom
talking to friends in foreign lands.

George E. Valler

I could chose my own entertainment
from a TV on the wall
everything I ever needed
at my beck and call.
Food, well that was plentiful
I could waste it all day long
and if it's not what I wanted
I would create a merry song.
School, was such a nuisance
It seemed so in the way
and takes away, precious time
that on my computer I could play
So then, will childhood be remembered
will my children want to know
there is an old, old saying
you reap all that you sow
So, as yesterday's child remembered
see the world as I could see
there's nothing now I cannot do
I just need to press a key

The curiosity of a child can be quite far reaching. My grandson was curious to visit a cemetery of all things and put him in rather a reflective mood.

Reflecting

We sat among the sleeping
from so many years ago.
The rain fell gently weeping
for all those we'll never know.

And peace was all around us
with the world we were at one.
Alone we sat together
with the setting of the sun.

We sat among the sleeping
they have no friend or foe
but the gates will soon be closing
so we must rise up and go.

CHAPTER 13

Do you remember that little poem earlier in the book, The Green Hill, all doom and gloom and the need for future planning, or else! We really need to give this old world some urgent consideration, well here is a more light-hearted poem that I wrote earlier with rather short verse.

Progress

There is a green hill far away
on which sits a cottage plot
but a builder one day came along
and bought the bleeding lot
then covered it with houses,
houses, all look the same
now that green hill far away
has lost its claim to fame

My wife, Patricia, otherwise known as, 'my good lady', has a group of like-minded ladies who meet up from time to time and go out on what they call, 'girls get-togethers' (usually extending to two days!). However, dancing celebrating, and general melee has to be paid for.

George E. Valler

Sound Sleep

Sound sleeps the beauty of the night
Seek out to hide from morning light
Rhythmic evening limbs do tell
Oh muscle-pain sends me to hell
Youth must I still have to seek
Ageless pain such sightless treat
This chase of youth I am of one
Lost to the dawn, have I not won
Darkness now I longer keep
As 'neath this blanket I now sleep

Sometimes words are not there. Many a writer has reason to worry, when this problem occurs, it can be quite daunting to say the least and you don't know if it is going to get better or leave you struggling. It's like falling into deep water, over your head, floundering, is it my day? Well I have been fortunate up to date, fingers crossed

Lost

I sit among the poet millions
my pen held in my hand
I watch the clock a ticking
I watch the movement of the hands

My mind it is in turmoil
the words I cannot make
the verse so easy, sometimes
seem now, to me, forsake

The sky no longer seeing
walking again the long lost road
my shoulder no longer a burden
to carry the long lost load

I have crossed rivers and crossed mountains
I have crossed the angry seas
yet words are not forthcoming
well could it then perhaps be me

My thoughts and words all doing time
blank is the space, blank is the rhyme
perhaps I'm just an empty space
my words now lost without a trace

But if I wait, then time may tell
and I will ring the writer's bell
my mind perhaps, just playing shock
could I then have had, the writer's block

Sorry, I'm still here, pen in hand, ink still wet, words still flowing, so where to next? How about a universal school, the poor old earth has given up, dust has descended upon us all, we are now a memory in the cosmos. Imagine a classroom and a teacher in the future.

The Universal Teacher

In a school somewhere in the universe
in the future, many moons ahead
a teacher needs a question asked

George E. Valler

from the history books they've read.
So tell me Johnny Mercury
or even Peter Mars
what do you see in our constellation
do you see in all our stars.
Where are all our planets
as they roll around the sun
and where they say that earth evolved
where they say, all life begun.
But this is now a lifeless waste
lost many years, we know
for reasons better known to man
with nowhere else to go.
It was, they say, a heaven
a heaven right there on earth
but man and all his wisdom
knew better, for what it's worth.
So a lifeless little heaven
now joins the celestial sky
and you have to ask the question
ask the question, why?
So you see now what can happen
don't let man decide your fate
we must then learn from history
why a heaven closed its gate.

Perhaps it was this that caused the problem, common sense in short supply. Now all is lost we have failed. Oh woe is me.

War, War And More

How foolish are the men of war
Have they not learnt from times before
From suffering all, such hate and pain
The road to nowhere left to gain.
They tear this world, this world apart
To only sorrow, break a heart
Young are the lives, no longer give
Young the life, no longer live
Destroy all before us, all will see
Power cries, just trust in me
I'll take you to these foreign lands
I'll change you boy, I'll make you man
To glory give, to glory die
Yours is not to ask the reason why.

But before all that happens let's get out the good old bottle of wine, brush off the garden table, roll out the garden chairs, sit back, relax, put all your worries behind you and enjoy.

The Garden

I smiled again this morning
as the sun peeped through the sky
The clouds they waved a hello
the wind greeted with a sigh
The lavender, her perfume
helped from the flowered rose
Made heaven in the garden
in the early morning throws
The bee in all her glory

seeks each flower's drooping head
A field mouse climbs a slender stalk
awakened from her early bed
The garden is the carpet
Nature lays out all before
We are only the keeper
Who paints the pictured floor

And if while you are drowsing in all this midday sun, wine closing those tired old eyes let's listen to nature's orchestra.

The Woodland

Sweet is the sound of bluebells
peel soft the winds delight
how yellow is the primrose dance
in the woodlands dewy night
The ivy caress her leafy twine
wild, the rose it's prickled smile
sweet violet splay her purple frock
linger on this floral isle

So how about me 'poet me'. How about a poem for me, or anyone else who feels they are a poet at heart, perhaps you may know someone. We all like to call ourselves 'A Poet' so let's not argue with that.

I am a Poet

How vain now is the poet
as he plays magic with his words

of sea, of sky, of you and I
no matter how absurd.
He'll sing songs of ships and ocean seas
of heaven, hell, so all believe
the pen will write, page after page
release the rhyme, strip clothes to rage.
The suffering pain he must describe
the reader kept in mind survived
lost in love, memories to time
with broken minds and city grime.
Pain and suffer, let words just start
never together, so shall we part
the daggered heart, sweet music make
the knife of life, cut slice the cake.
Come us, just gather, make the crowd
Let Church bells ring, oh poet proud.

Can I follow on with another poem on poets. We all think that authors are rich. 'Wow, you have written a book, what's it called, is it exciting'. Could be!

Poets Lament

If my words make me a rich man
though my pockets may be bare
my words I can just throw around
in my words I need not care

For if they earn me not a penny
they are there for all to share
if to ears my words bring joy at least
release memories to compare

George E. Valler

So my pockets may be empty
if it's words I have in my head
how sweet the sound my ringing words
give to me my daily bread

Let hunger sharp, the written word
turn to hope that history shows
for in pain and all such suffering
doth the beauty ring in prose

Well perhaps the final fall at the first hurdle, as a budding author, you have tried your best, you have written your heart on your sleeve and then.

Time To Ponder

I thought I would be a poet
after all I know my A B C
and if I string a few words together
well just how hard can that really be.
Shall I write a few words or a sonnet
put something down that will rhyme
how many verses should I ponder
at the end will I really have time.
Think of all the money I'll be making
when my masterpiece, I will publish
I'll send off loads of submissions
but my work all comes back - rubbish!

At this moment shall we go back a little in time. If you remember some of the old TV game shows, from Blankety Blank's cheque book and pen to the possibility of a million pounds with Chris Tarrant in the chair.

Who Wants To Be a ....

Today it's the quiz shows
that are all the trend
from stopping the clock
to 'phoning a friend.

I've got your mate Dez
on the end of the line
the next voice you hear
will be his and not mine.

The question you'll ask
for the audience don't know
is 'where in Alaska
would you expect to find snow?'.

He'll give you the answer
pick one leaving three
then when you have finished
you'll come back to me.

The clock's started counting
there's a minute to go
'where the hell is Alaska?
where the hell is the snow?'.

Sorry, time's up
the clock's got you beaten

George E. Valler

which school did you go to
was it Oxford or Eton!

You still have a lifeline
you can take away two
by the look on your face
you haven't a clue!

Come on, make your mind up,
final answer I'll take
then we'll see if it's right
straight after the break.

If you'd said' IN Alaska'
you'd expect to find snow
you'd be sitting here still
now you're having to go.

So come on now audience
give him a big hand
for he still goes away
but not quite as he planned.

CHAPTER 14

On holiday quite recently and dropping into a pub, 'The Smithy' it was called and on the wall they had blacksmith memorabilia. If you remember earlier in the book I wrote a blacksmith poem. I offered them my poem, and they, delighted, displayed it on the wall with the rest. I just had to write a response.

The Smithy Pub.

In a Smithy Pub in Lancashire
among the bric-a-brac on the wall
there hangs a blacksmith's memory
from our history we can recall.
With the hot coals of his furnace
he could turn his hand, was often said,
to hammer out his iron trade
upon an anvils steely bed.
But the future overtook him
passed by his willing hand
his services no longer
no longer in demand.
The shed no longer standing
the coals no longer hot
he's just a village memory
now lost, to be forgot.

I must admit I sometimes take a liking to a particular way words can express, 'to hammer out his iron trade upon an anvil's steely bed"

George E. Valler

When I first met Patricia, my good lady, many moons ago I could never imagine my good fortune, where had she come from, how was it that it was me. Perhaps you may have had the same thoughts, or perhaps not!

Just Tonight

You are that pretty lady
That I met up with just tonight
With flowing hair and beauty look
So dainty trip in evening light.
Our first hello when eyes we met
Such moments one cannot forget
That night, oh, so long ago
Remembered still as memories show.
You were the night turned into day
Forever now, the years we stay
That pretty lady of the past
Where oft we thought, too good to last.
Sit now my side, this day is here
And time will toll another year
Together still life's ship we sail
So once again another tale.
You are that pretty lady
That I met up with, just tonight

Just a simple three verse poem of hope and freedom. With so many troubles in the world today, as always, maybe you'll like this

Freedom

Walk me down the road to freedom
Where the peaceful waters lie
Where the hearts are still unbroken
Where the children never cry

Where the flags of hope are flying
Where our dreams can never die
Where the streets are paved with love
No questions asked or reasons why

Where as one can we together
Down this road we wish to go
Where the milk of human kindness
Seems to forever flow.

I was in need of an operation. It would appear that my left shoulder was not up to every day happenings and a surgeon was to replace my shoulder with a nice new shiny one. There are many of us roaming around with spare parts. The operation was something else and when I could remember after the mist of the anaesthetic wore off - I just had to write.

The Dark

How dance must you upon my bed
Needs rest must I my weary head
Oh nurse must you my prison hold
My saviour yes, as be so bold
Suffered pain is want of me

George E. Valler

Muscle torn, torn limb agree
Deep dread the surgeon knife I flee
Cut deep the blade, my dreams cut me
Nurse dance must you upon my bed
Dark is the night, my bed must rest
Change your way, of me leave free
As psychedelic dreams chase me
Oh return of me from hellish night
Day doth dawn, tells of my plight
Onward, forward day must dread
No dance must you upon my bed.

Let's get away from operations and pain, let's talk holidays or what you can do on holiday. I find I can do much more reading, perhaps because one has more time. Having read two or three I thought about the books I have read in the past, and forgotten the story. A little nonsense poem about just that.

Memory of a Book

There's just one book upon my shelf
But I haven't read it yet
For when I read it all before
I somehow then forget

If a second book that I should have
Have I read it all before?
For looking at my bookshelf
Why on earth would I want more

Let my shelf then be empty, free,
With no books all in a row
For then I would have read them
Of that I would not know

So I'll take my one book off the shelf
To read then just feel free
Because I can't remember reading it
The suspense is killing me!

Talking of books, here is another book that needs some recognition
left all alone sitting on a desk. Is there hope, of course.

The Lost Legend

There's a Collins English Dictionary
it sits upon my desk.
The fountain of printed knowledge
should I need to put it to the test.

The book is A to Z and heavy
with meaning on every page.
But information looking up
now lost to the modern age.

For Google in its infinite
is but a fingertip away.
With everything you need to know
everything you need to say.

George E. Valler

It's all there in the airwaves
printing for the modern age.
With words just flashed before you
no need to turn another page.

But should there come a time
when electronics shuts the door.
Then my Collins English Dictionary
could then come to the fore.

How about a silly little short verse

Little Old Lady

She sits rocking in her rollers
she sits rocking in her chair.
She is rocking through her memories
she hasn't got a rocking care.
The children have gone rocking
they're rocking all away.
The only worry now she has
They might come back to rocking stay!

It would appear that in poetry there are a variety of ways, directions, stanzas, etc. but to me I like a poem to roll along and entertain. How you can bounce off each word, whether it's two or four, if it has bounce, it has rhythm, it has 'It'.

A Wedding

Church bells sound, organ plays
The day is bright, the sun it's rays
The bride her dreams, now all in white
Unsteady groom, the fallen night
Vows all read, now all set
No time now, no time regret
Empty glass in wine will pour
For empty glass, require more
Speeches made, words all said
Discarded paper, words now read
Cake is cut, save one a slice
Taking home, don't ask twice
Left, we dance the night to pass
In wine will pour an empty glass
Together off, distance away
Married now so start the day
Honeymoon they know the score
That door was opened way before
Stand now must I on falling gate
Not stagger now, is it too late
Empty glass in wine will pour
For empty glass requires more
Night over now, enough said
I need to seek a softened bed
For empty glass in wine will pour
For empty glass requires more

When I was very young and at school, my one ambition was to be an apprentice jockey. All my school work was based on horses and jockeys. All my drawings were of horses. When I left school I went into a racing stable. Three disillusioned years later, with my call-up papers in my hand, I could with the greatest of pleasure leave those memories behind. But in later years my daughter's interest in horses put me back into the saddle. So I expect there was some benefit to be had. In recognition of man's most loyal subject - the horse.

War Horse

He throws his head he stamps his feet
For him there is then no retreat
The man of war he carries
To the drums relentless beat.
Into the wall of death he gallops
Pushed by spurs upon his side
His pain and suffering all is lost
To satisfy mans vanity and pride.
He did not ask he had no choice
The horse obeys he has no voice
His time is now he's mans best friend
And loyal he serves the bitter end.

Also, as a young boy I was an avid churchgoer and chorister and even graduated into becoming a server, looking after the wine for the vicar as he slurped his way through the service. I was bought up to believe (as most of us were) that goodness would be rewarded in heaven and of course the opposite, I would be shovelling for the devil.

Such is Life

When I was a child and mother put me to bed
I always remembered the words that she said.

Be righteous and pure and do always your best
for life is a journey and God's earthly test.

And if I was good up to heaven I would go
but if I was bad, to the fires down below.

So I went off to school as I knew that I should
and did all the things that made me so good.

I went often to church and learnt how to pray
and did all the right things one should every day.

For if I was good up to heaven I would go
and if I was bad, to the fires down below.

I helped charities for children, old ladies cross the road,
discovered the Rotary, campaigned for the toad.

Through the years I have travelled doing nothing but good
and it would in heaven that I'd be understood.

So if I was good up to heaven I would go
and if I was bad, to the fires down below.

Now I've done all I could for my fellow man
so helping to shape my eternal plan.

George E. Valler

Time here now has ended, I've met my demise
church singing my praises as they look to the skies.

Well, if I was good up to heaven I would go
And if I was bad, to the fires down below.

This life now I'm leaving in Ad Memoriam
Oh no!   Where am I going!

That's the Crematorium.

CHAPTER 15

Rubbish is the scourge of our life, paper, scattering the glorious countryside, ending up in tips to be either incinerated or even into landfill. Holding hands with its infamous partner the dreaded plastic of all sorts, but.........

The Crumpled Piece of Paper

There's a crumpled piece of paper
That's lying upon your bed
There's not much you can do with it
After all that's what is said
But if a pen could write upon it
It would open a brand new world
With many a wondrous moment
Many a moment to be unfurled
It could take you to those foreign lands
Unfold many a dream gone by
It could take you to your heartaches
Help you to say goodbye
So spare a thought for that crumpled paper
Before you throw it in the bin
For you could write upon it
A Masterpiece - so now begin

We haven't said anything about God have we. I know it can be a touchy subject but one can ask questions can't one? As I have said earlier I was into the church, in the choir, Sunday school in the afternoon after morning service, now many years older I have a different outlook on religion and its outpourings. My poem, Such Is Life, earlier in the book, took a rather more amusing look at our religious teachings, but let's take a more serious look.

God and Hope

If God was such a caring soul
Would we be in this mess
Would we be more loving people
Not suffer this distress

How can you believe in anything
How can it all be right
If all that seems to happen
We suffer the devil's might

When you raise the flag of freedom
Whose side are you then on
You cannot be doing right
If forever you are doing wrong

It would seem that God is chaos
With someone else to blame
For what would be one man's loss
Is another man's, then, gain

For if there is a heaven on earth
Many then would disagree
The hands of life tied behind the back
How can anyone then feel free

The good, the bad, the ugly
Life seems to embrace it all
Maybe we should resign ourselves
Toss the dice and let it fall

Now how about when the time comes and you are stood at the bus stop to oblivion, next stop, well, if you are on the Devil's express, someone waiting for you, let's go and visit old Lucifer.

A Dream

I dreamt I died the other night
But it wasn't all that bad
And with this pain and suffering gone
Of that, well I was glad
Old Lucifer bought me a cup of tea
Boiled on his cauldron of fire
Saying, how's it going up there
Just thought I would enquire
I said it's getting rather chaotic
So many religions, spoilt for choice
He smiled and looked at me again
Dear boy, in the end there's just one voice
Come let me show you around
So you can get to know the place
Forget all your troubles up there
You no longer have to chase
I've set aside a shovel
And a place for you to reside
No need to introduce your friends
They're all down here by your side

George E. Valler

We work a twelve hour shift down here
Working throughout the night
For now up there they've stopped using coal
The demand is getting rather light
Tea is served each morning
After the work's been done
Unfortunately, now you are down here
You no longer will see the sun
But it does have its compensations
It's really quite nice and warm
No longer need you worry
About the gathering of the storm
Just think you are so lucky
You could be stuck up in the clouds
Playing the harp all day
Dressed in that awful shroud
The daytime then is left to you
To ponder on what you had
I think that then you will agree
This Hell is not so bad

So, now take my hand dear reader, no not literally, poetically, let's visit the Arts, the magic of the brush. 'The hallowed halls of history hanging on the walls of time'

The Gallery

Is this a Geovaller that I am seeing
Yes, that is a Geovaller, quite sure
But how can you tell it's his painting
Why so certain, tell me more

My Life in The Poetry Lane

You can tell it's a Geovaller by looking
The way the brush strokes just flow
The curve in the smile, such a blessing
Even the shape of the nose

The colours demand one's attention
The figures seem to call out, hello
How the light, such glorious reflection
It's like no one else that I know

He's up there with Batiste and Caravaggio
Even likened to Messier le Rembrandt
They say his portrayal of a garden
Would take a life time of wine to decant

So dear lady, is the Geovaller of interest
Could you see it hanging on your wall
It's a picture ideal for hanging
Perhaps somewhere in your hall

A picture then like no other
It's expensive, the price you can see
But if madam would like it gift wrapped
The Gallery will deliver it free

May I ask madam, why such an interest
Have you seen a Geovaller before
Yes, I married the b****** didn't I
Now I just need a mat for the door

CHAPTER 16

The little semi cottage that we lived in throughout the war was so limited in size to house all of us comfortably. My mother a strong little lady consistently badgered the local town council reminding them of our needs (like so many others) and on what rung of the ladder could we be on, with each visit. Her persistence paid off and we were given the keys to a brand new house in a village not far away. The village was small to say the least. It did not have any shops but did boast a pub, 'an old boy's retreat'. Outside this pub called by the unusual name of 'The Shears' was a convenient bench, the bench became the meeting place of four old retired gents who would sit with their pot of ale and reminisce as the world rolled by. Then one day I noticed only three now sat on the bench, then on a later occasion only two old gents. One day the bench became empty and had been taken over by a couple of Hippies. The old gents one by one had died until the bench became vacant, a little reminder of the village and its past so I wrote The Four Musketeers.

The Four Musketeers

Gentlemen, we meet
are we not The Four Musketeers.
Outside the ale house now we sit
drinking in those golden years.

George E. Valler

This bench it is our historic throne
remembering long this village life.
As we survey then all before
all the troubles and the strife.

But our autumn years are with us
seeds of life fall from the tree.
Then, for whom the bell tolls
are we left, we only three.

But still we meet and reminisce
the sun, the sky, deep blue.
So soon again the bell will toll
and leave just only two.

The seat now, lost and empty
Musketeers, gone, all their years.
And memories forgotten now
no longer shed the tears.

The village has moved on again
moved into a distant, new.
Memories walk a faster step
was there four, then three, then two.

Today I am reminded of good fortune living in this moment in time and as I look out of my window, the postman, bag hanging off his shoulder and despite the weather, cool and drizzling rain, our postman has the obligatory (or so it seems) shorts. All our postmen are now wearing shorts. Time to post a postman poem.

Bare Leg Shorts

The postman in his bare leg shorts
walking in the rain
accepting the discomfort
accepting all the pain
Walking with his heavy load
pushing letters through the slot
he has to keep on walking
until he's posted all the lot
Then its off back to the depot
to get out of the pouring rain
but then there comes another bag
and he has to do it all again

I am now long retired and looking out of my front-room window, waiting in anticipation for the postman to come, but for some people the postman doesn't stop.

Waiting

I sit in front of my window
looking out across the road
waiting for the postman
carrying his heavy load.

The rattle of the letter box
cards falling upon the floor
but the postman with his heavy load
just walks right past my door.

George E. Valler

I look back out the window
now so quiet and so still
then in my hand I raise my pen
and, smiling, sign my Will.

Remembering the past can be quite daunting, with man and his relentless pursuit of Devil and Disaster, terrifying experiences come to pass, such is the horror man can inflict upon his fellow man. The whole world remembers the unbelievable 911 happening when we all watched in complete disbelief as the TV played out the horrendous moments as they happened right before our eyes.
I give you.

Sad September.

They came in on a wing
their captives in prayer
they had gone beyond life
they had gone beyond care

Their aim to impact
such a symbol of power
to topple the face
of a financial tower

They took them, the innocent
on their journey of hate
in the misguided belief
that their cause was so great

For whatever reason
ask, what did they gain

to leave such a legacy
of bitterness and pain

With memories created
engulfed all in flames
and no one wanting
to take on the blame

Was it all done for nothing
what was their aim
to commit those in their thousands
to suffering in vain

Has it now changed forever
the way that we live
for what we have received
we now have to give

The world is divided
but how can we tell
which path is to heaven
which path is to hell

Do you think life is a lottery, spin the wheel, just let it stop. Well just remember, life is an instant, in the aeons of time we are of given moments.

Given Moments

These few moments we are given
these few moments here on earth

George E. Valler

and yet it seems a lifetime
a lifetime for what it's worth
so what have you done with it
what have you done everyday
that you can look back upon
have you really had your say
what did you do tomorrow
was yesterday the same
did all your moments just appear
was there someone else to blame
or did you take life by the scruff
made every moment count
a helping hand you offered
gave each moment without doubt
were you a tower of virtue
were you one to aspire
perhaps that better person
singing in life's celestial choir
or were you just a ragamuffin
an all round layabout
whose world owed you a living
all against you without doubt
well I must admit it takes all kind
for life was given, come what may
perhaps you need to think about
why not, how nice the day

Now let us finish our brief moment together, wrap up our journey with.

My Life in The Poetry Lane

Moments we are given.

Be it five or ten or twenty
time will keep ahead the score
as we climb the stairs to nowhere
and close life's open door
a page perhaps in history
lost in the time of past
the road for now, oblivion
is all that we can ask
but this brief moment we are given
to do with as we wish
in this vast eternal never land
we have had our own brief kiss
the steps of time we've wandered
grateful surely then must be
for five or ten or twenty
remember as a memory

ENCORE

That was going to be the end of our little journey but since you have stayed with me this far, how about I give you an encore as if I were an entertainer. I walk off the page and then return to your applause (hopefully!) and offer you a final taste of poetry in rhyme.

Do you remember earlier in the book we mentioned the cycling widow and 'you know what', well what if she has given it some thought.

We now have a sequel.

The Cycling Widow

When it comes to the bike and me
well me and, you know what!
perhaps I could make him reconsider
put him right on the spot.
So I will join his blasted cycling club
and wear Lycra like a banner
so he knows what he can do
what he can do with his blasted spanner.
I could cycle up and down
even do the turkey trot
and get him all in a lather
thinking, perhaps, well you know what!

George E. Valler

I'll join his blasted cycling club
cycle around with all his mates
and when we go cross country
I'll show him just what it takes.
And when it comes to peddling
and I am in the queue
with my bottom bobbing up and down
I could really spoil his view.
But will it get him around to thinking
thinking, well, you know what!
or will it get, oh god, the others,
all the others, thinking, you know what!
Perhaps I had better reconsider
think again, about my manner
go out into that blasted shed
and help him hold his spanner.

You ladies I find amazing, how often do you stand in front of a mirror. My wife would not go out without makeup. Have you thought how many hours in your life are spent on makeup time. That hidden beauty made to shine. You say that you do it for yourself, your own esteem. But it's also for us.

The Mirror

As I look into the mirror
the reflection that I see
the face that now walks with me
for all the world to see

A face that smiled a thousand smiles
the face to show a thousand frowns

a face that looks at all the world
in all its ups and downs

A sorrowed look, said with a sigh
the pain that shows a sad goodbye
eyes that reflect, a tear drop flows
to mask a pain that never shows

A face that asked, will you be mine
and always be my valentine
a face that kissed with passion lips
a hankie face, a nose that drips

A face now weathered over time
moments reflect in every line
the salted sea, life's watered brine
reflect now mirror, yes it's mine

If you feel that all that has failed, don't worry my next poem will give you solace.

Let's Face It

If a face could launch a thousand ships
how many then could sink with mine.
If I was on prison release
I would ask to do more time.
Life has not been kind to me
it hasn't helped one little bit.
I even had the Devil ask
as a model, would I sit.

George E. Valler

The bathroom is my saving grace
hidden behind swirling steam.
where in the mirror I can look
I can look and only dream.
Don't wipe away that image
leave me some little hope.
That life within the daylight
can give me room to cope.
But I know there is a someone
who knows me oh so well.
Who is more than pleased to see me
of that I can always tell.
All he asks is a nice warm bed
in the corner of the floor.
And a lead, that's hanging on a hook
swinging on the old back door.

Food is always on our minds, as I mentioned at the start of our journey, the pie man in our village. A friend of mine once wrote that he had sat down to enjoy a jam and cream scone and that a scone had to be just perfect. I gave this some thought. What if the scone wasn't perfect. Try a taste of my scone - what do you think?

The Scone

How sweet is this
the jammy taste
how soft the enclosed flour
the fruitiness of speckled mix
brings joy the tasting hour.
But wrong does then the baking play
create a moment new

for poorly bake and poorly taste
go back into the memory queue

The pandemic has left us to get on with our lives. Did it do us any favours? It tortured a few, gave us a whole lot of trouble, left a lot of us reeling. I give you a reminder.

School's Out

No child now in the classroom
no child to sing or shout
no shoes scuffing in the playground
no children running round about.
The teachers they are long gone
the school, locked up in time
the silence that surrounds it
somehow really seems a crime.
The child now sits at home
with little else to do
while teachers have just disappeared
left to cope, there are a few.
There are a thousand reasons why
 there is no one left in class.
The pandemic is the teacher.
Oh how long before it's passed.

and finally

George E. Valler

Modern Man

The aeroplanes are up and flying
the cars gone back to work
and if global warming matters
don't put a bet upon your shirt

The smoke stacks still keep smoking
even at pounds and pounds a pack
and lads down on the corner
they will still be selling crack

Waste still remains a problem
as it lies scattered on the floor
so if the time it ever happens
can't we just sit back and close a door

For after all I am quite happy
living life the way I am
if no one else seems bothered
why should I really give a damn

Eighteen months I've worn a mask
seen people dying by the score
and just when things are getting back
you come to me and ask for more

I can't go planting Amazon trees
or trawling plastic from the sea
I'm not built for all that hard work
it's an easy life for me

My Life in The Poetry Lane

Perhaps next year I might consider
when someone else has done it all
if then perhaps you still need me
feel free, give me a call

My life in the Poetry lane

ONE MORE TIME ....

OK, what about some random thoughts

There are two sides to a coin, a tail and a head,
but the value's the same when all else is said

Oh what a tangled bed we leave when first we practice to conceive

----

I am but half my children but they are all of me

In the beginning the world was created and so began both heaven and hell

----

Invisible is the ink that writes the missing word

George E. Valler

Waste not your love on a nobody, therein, no value lies

Now is the weather and our discontent
Made glorious summer by a trip to York

I wandered lonely as a cloud and then it rained!

Thank you, dear reader, we've come to the end of the Lane and I hope you have enjoyed the journey.

George

The Author